W9-DJG-813

RosettaStone®
Language Learning · Success

User's Guide | Levels 1 & 2

TRS-UG-ENG-2.0.7
ISBN 1-58022-022-3

Printed in the United States of America

Fairfield Language Technologies
135 West Market Street
Harrisonburg, Virginia 22801 USA

Telephone: 540-432-6166 or 800-788-0822 in U.S. and Canada
Fax: 540-432-0953
E-mail: info@RosettaStone.com
Web site: www.RosettaStone.com

Table of Contents

1.0 Getting Started

Welcome to the Rosetta Stone Language Library! The User's Guide is designed to help you answer specific questions about running the Rosetta Stone. You can learn about how the program is set up, what kinds of special features are available, and how to customize the Lessons to fit your needs.

In the User's Guide, you can go directly to a specific topic. Or, you can use the text as a general guide as you work your way through the program.

How to Use this Text

The User's Guide is divided into four general categories:

1. Getting Started

2. Program Operation

3. System Preferences

4. Reference

The information is broken into topics within these general categories. Every topic has a reference number that indicates its place in the book's structure.

The Table of Contents lists all categories and their reference numbers; the Index (4.5) gives page numbers.

Example of numbering system

> 3. System Preferences
> 3.1 User Options Tab
> 3.1.2 Logging In

You can also access this text in electronic form by clicking on the Help button, located in the lower right corner of every screen. When you click on the Help button, you will be taken directly to the Help section(s) concerning the screen with which you are working.

For more on how to use the On-Screen Help Text, click on the Help button (2.12) and follow the link at the top of any page in the On-Screen Help Text.

The Glossary of Terms & Icons (4.4) contains definitions of common terms and descriptions of icon functions.

In this Section

Section 1, Getting Started, introduces you to the Rosetta Stone's method and structure. It also provides a step-by-step guide to installing and running the program.

1.1 The Rosetta Stone Method

1.2 Program Overview

1.3 Installing and running the Rosetta Stone

> For technical support information, see section 4.3.

1.1 The Rosetta Stone Method

The Rosetta Stone program is designed to teach you a new language the way you learned your first language: by directly associating words—written and spoken—with objects, actions and ideas that convey meaning. The Rosetta Stone uses pictures to establish the meaning of words and phrases so that there is no translation. Grammar, syntax, and vocabulary are taught through real-life examples. You know what a word means because you have associated it with the meaning directly (communicated through pictures) rather than with the same word in your own language. You do not need to depend on translation, lengthy explanations of grammar, or memorization drills. This encourages the development of inherent language skills that equip you to communicate in context.

The Rosetta Stone uses Dynamic Immersion, a method that simulates a real-life immersion experience and relies on your active participation. All Lessons are taught in the target language, quickly developing your ability to understand the spoken and written language. Tasks and activities keep you involved in the learning process. Speaking and Writing Exercises help you develop correct pronunciation and spelling. Different Modes allow you to re-create the pacing of real life conversation. Grammar is taught through usage and patterns throughout the majority of the program; it is taught explicitly in Level 3, in the target language as Narrative Lessons. Throughout the program, new information is presented systematically so that words or grammatical forms are easily identified and understood.

With the Rosetta Stone, you learn more than syntax and vocabulary. While using the program, you develop language-learning strategies that will help you in any context, at any point in language development. Instead of translation and memorization, you learn how to depend on your own skills of pattern-recognition, correlation, deduction, and induction, just as you would in a real conversation. These are strategies you already use, drawing from context to figure out an unfamiliar word, recognizing root words, and inferring meaning even if the grammar is not familiar.

The primary goal of the Rosetta Stone method is two-fold: to help you learn a language quickly, easily, and correctly, and to equip you with the strategies and confidence that will aid your understanding and communication in the real world.

1.2 Program Overview

This section will give you an idea of the structure of the Rosetta Stone. You can see how the different elements of the program are connected. The section also contains recommendations for how to work through the program in your first session. All of these features are discussed in more detail throughout the book.

The structure of the Rosetta Stone allows you to focus on a manageable section of information—a Lesson. Your choices of Language, Product, and Unit will determine which Lesson you work with. The Language Skills, Preview, Guided Exercises, regular Exercises, Tests, and Modes are all different ways of working with the Lesson material.

To get started:

Language
Spanish
English
French
etc.

• Click on the Language (2.2)

Product
Level 1
Level 2
Level 3

• Click on on the Product (2.2)

Unit
Picture
Video (Level 3)
Narrative (Level 3)

• Click on Unit 1 (2.3)

Lesson
1, 2, 3, 4...

• Click on Lesson 1 (2.4)

Language Skill
A: Listening and Reading
B: Listening
C: Reading
D: Speaking
E: Writing

• Click on Language Skill A: Listening and Reading (2.6)

Preview   **Guided Exercise**   **Test**

Exercise
Exercise 1   *Exercise 2*
Exercise 3   *Exercise 4*

Modes
Delay
Timer

You can work with the Lesson material in several different way:

• Click Preview (2.7) if you want to study the answers.

• Click Guided Exercises (2.8) if you want to work through the Lesson material using a prescribed sequence of Preview and Exercise activities.

• Click one of the Exercises (2.9) if you want to work with a Lesson using a specific combination of text, speech, and pictures in a scored, question/answer activity.

• Click on the Test icon (2.10) and choose an Exercise if you know the material well, and would like to test yourself.

• Click on the Modes (2.11) to modify an Exercise or a Test.

1.3 Installing and Running the Rosetta Stone

This section explains the initial steps of using the Rosetta Stone:

1. Installing the application.
2. Running the application with the language data disc.

Step 1. Installing the Rosetta Stone application

Insert the application disc.

- In some cases (Demo), the application and language data are on a single disc. If you did not receive a separate application CD-ROM, insert the language data disc and follow the instructions below.

Depending on your system, an Autorun screen will appear.

If the Autorun screen appears:

- Click on Install.
- Click on Run Installer.
- Follow the directions on the screen to complete the installation.
- Go to Step 2: Running the application with the language data disc.

If the Autorun screen does not appear, follow the directions below:

> All of this information is also located at www.RosettaStone.com/home/support/installing. If you have further questions, contact Technical Support (4.3).

Windows Users:

- Click on "Start" in your computer's taskbar.
- Point to Settings.
- Click on "Control Panel" in the Settings submenu.
- In the Control Panel, click on "Add/Remove Programs."
- For Windows XP, click on the "Add New Programs" button, then on the "CD or Floppy" button. In previous versions of Windows, click "Install" from the "Install/Uninstall" tab to begin the installation.
- Follow the on-screen instructions to complete the installation.

  Windows will find the SETUP.EXE installation program on the CD-ROM.

Mac OS Users:

- Double-click the icon named The Rosetta Stone Installer.
- Click on the install button.
- When the installer is done, click Quit.

For all systems:

- Install Apple QuickTime for Windows and Adobe Acrobat Reader as needed.

  QuickTime is used to view video clips in select Demo, Level 2, and Level 3 lessons.

  Adobe Acrobat Reader is needed to read the User's Guide in the Docs folder on the Application CD-ROM.

> **Note:** If your computer does not have QuickTime 5.0 or higher installed on its hard drive, then the Rosetta Stone installer will begin an automatic update of QuickTime. The QuickTime installer will ask you for a registration number. **You do not need this for the Rosetta Stone Products.** Simply leave the registration number field blank and click "Next" to continue with the installation.

Step 2. Running the Application with the Language Data Disc

Windows Users:

Take out the application disc (if used) and insert the language data disc into the CD-ROM drive.

Double-click on "The Rosetta Stone" icon on your desktop or follow these directions:

• Click "Start" on the Windows task bar, usually located in the lower left corner of the screen.

• Select "Programs."

• Select The Rosetta Stone Program Folder.

• Click on "The Rosetta Stone" icon.

Mac OS Users:

Take out the application disc (if used) and insert the language data disc into the CD-ROM drive.

• Open your computer's hard drive.

• Open the Applications folder.

  If you are using Mac OS X and a version of the Rosetta Stone that requires the Mac Classic environment, open the "Applications (Mac OS 9)" folder.

• Double-click on "The Rosetta Stone" icon.

1.3.1 Uninstalling the Program

Windows Users have three options for uninstalling the program:

Option 1: Click the "Uninstall" button in the Autorun screen.

Option 2:

• Click on "Start" in the Windows task bar.

• Select "Programs."

• Select "The Rosetta Stone."

• Click on "Uninstall the Rosetta Stone."

Option 3:

• Click on "Start" in the Windows task bar.

• Select "Settings."

• Click on "Control Panel."

• Double-click on "Add/Remove Programs."

• Select The Rosetta Stone Program Folder.

• Click "Remove."

Mac OS Users:

Simply drag The Rosetta Stone folder into the trash. Make sure to throw away any aliases you may have created.

2.0 Program Operation

This section explains how to use the Rosetta Stone program.

You will learn:

• how the program is structured.

• about options for learning and reviewing material.

• how to use each feature.

2.1 Menu Screen

The Menu screen appears after you log in.

To log in (3.1.1) or change the program settings (3.0) click on the settings button:

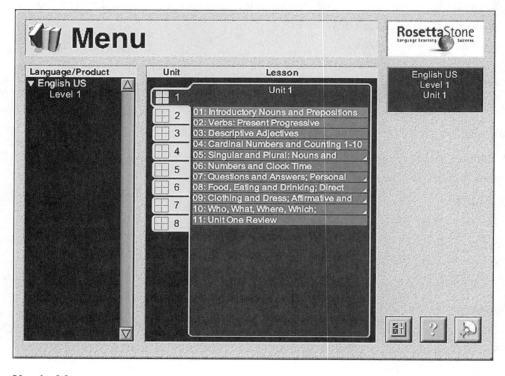

Use the Menu screen to:

• click on the Language, Product, Unit, and Lesson you wish to use.

• move from one Unit or Lesson to another.

When you return to the Menu screen, the last Unit and Lesson you worked on will be highlighted.

2.2 Languages and Products

A list of available Languages (English, Spanish, Chinese, etc.) and Products (Level 1, Level 2, Level 3, etc.) is located on the left side of the Menu screen.

- Click the Language you wish to learn.
- Then select a Product.
- The available Units and Lessons will appear on the middle of the Menu screen.

2.3 Units

Units are listed by number to the right of the Languages and Products.

- Click a Unit icon to see the Lessons taught in that particular Unit.

2.4 Lessons

Units are divided into 5-12 Lessons which are listed in the middle of the Menu screen.

The material in each Lesson builds on language previously learned, allowing you to proceed systematically through the program.

- Click the title of the Lesson you wish to start. This will take you to the Activities screen.

These Lessons use pictures, text, and sound to teach comprehension and production of phrases, sentences, and short dialogues. A Picture Lesson has forty pictures with corresponding texts. The picture/text pairs are grouped in sets of four; these sets are called quads. Within a Lesson, Exercises use different combinations of the pictures, spoken text, and written text to teach meaning, pronunciation, writing and/or reading. There are ten quads in each Picture Lesson.

To learn more, see Language Skills (2.6) and Picture Exercises (2.9.1 – 2.9.3).

2.5 Activities Screen

The Activities screen appears when you select a Lesson (2.4). The options in the Activities screen allow you to work through the Lesson material several times in a variety of ways.

Use the Activities screen to choose:

- Language Skills (2.6)
- Preview (2.7)
- Guided Exercises (2.8)
- Exercises (2.9)
- Test (2.10)
- Two Modes (2.11) can be used with Exercises and Tests:
  Timer (2.11.1)
  Delay (2.11.2)

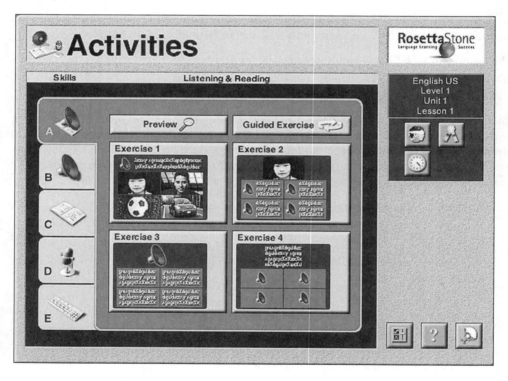

Use the Activities screen to:

- choose or change how the Lesson material is presented to you.
- focus on different Language Skills (listening, reading, speaking, writing).
- tailor the program to your needs and goals.

2.6 Language Skills

The Lesson material can be used to develop all the Language Skills: Listening and Reading, Listening, Reading, Speaking, and Writing. The first three Language Skills emphasize comprehension, while the last two emphasize production.

- Click a Language Skill tab, located on the left side of the Activities screen (2.5), to see the available Exercises in the Language Skill.

Language Skill A: Listening and Reading

- Associates meaning directly with spoken and written words and phrases
- Teaches the correlation between spoken and written language
- Develops reading skills
- Develops listening comprehension

Language Skill B: Listening

- Develops comprehension of spoken language
- Associates meaning with spoken words and phrases

Language Skill C: Reading

- Develops comprehension of written language
- Associates meaning with written words and phrases

Language Skill D: Speaking

- Allows you to compare your speech with that of a native speaker
- Teaches pronunciation and inflection
- Reinforces listening skills

Language Skill E: Writing

- Improves spelling, capitalization, punctuation, vocabulary, and syntax
- Reinforces listening skills
- Reinforces meaning of words

2.7 Preview

The Preview allows you to see and hear the text matched with the correct picture. You can also practice reading and listening comprehension, and pronunciation.

You can access the Preview in two ways:

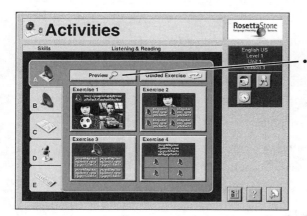

• Click on the Preview button in the Activities screen.

OR

• In an Exercise, use the Preview/Exercise toggle, located in the Control Panel (2.12). Click the Preview button (right) to enter Preview. Click the Exercise button (left) to resume the Exercise.

Because the Preview is intended for practice and study, score is not kept. Evaluate your knowledge and skills with the Guided Exercises, the Exercises, and the Tests. For more on score, see Control Panel (2.12).

You can also use the Preview to reinforce individual Language Skills.

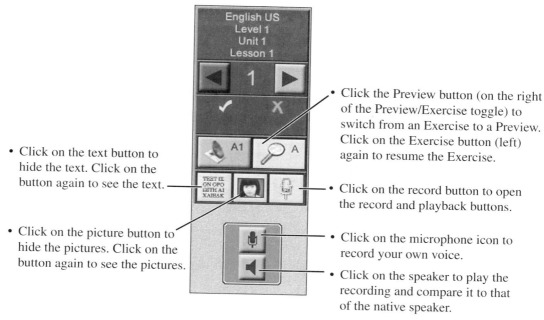

• Click on the text button to hide the text. Click on the button again to see the text.

• Click the Preview button (on the right of the Preview/Exercise toggle) to switch from an Exercise to a Preview. Click on the Exercise button (left) again to resume the Exercise.

• Click on the record button to open the record and playback buttons.

• Click on the picture button to hide the pictures. Click on the button again to see the pictures.

• Click on the microphone icon to record your own voice.

• Click on the speaker to play the recording and compare it to that of the native speaker.

2.8 Guided Exercise

The Guided Exercise is a prescribed sequence of Preview and Exercise activities for the Lesson and Language Skill you have selected. If you give an incorrect answer, the program will return to that quad or comprehension question throughout the Lesson until you get all four answers correct on the first try.

To do a Guided Exercise:

• Click on the Guided Exercise button in the Activities screen: `Guided Exercise`
• Study and respond as in a regular Exercise.

2.9 Exercises

In the Activities screen (2.5), click a Language Skill tab (2.6) to see the available Exercises.

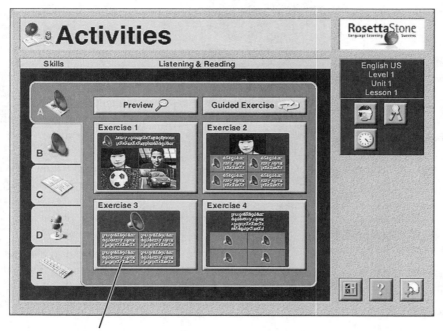

Click an Exercise button to open the corresponding Exercise. Exercises use quads—combinations of text, sounds, and pictures—to develop specific Language Skills:

Language Skill A: Listening and Reading

Language Skill B: Listening

Language Skill C: Reading

Language Skill D: Speaking

Language Skill E: Writing

For all Language Skills in all Units, the Exercise buttons show which combination of text, sounds, and pictures make up the prompts and response boxes.

Note: The Rosetta Stone offers many Exercises to accommodate a variety of learning styles and goals. It is not intended for you to complete every Exercise. Instead, focus on those which suit your learning style and help you accomplish your personal objectives.

2.9.1 Picture Exercises for Language Skill A: Listening and Reading; Language Skill B: Listening; and Language Skill C: Reading

To do an Exercise:

- Study the prompt given in the upper part of the screen.

  It can be:

  - spoken text.
  - written text.
  - a picture.
  - a combination of the above.

- Click the response option at the bottom of the screen that corresponds with the prompt.

  Response options can be:

  - spoken text.
  - written text.
  - a picture.
  - a combination of the above.

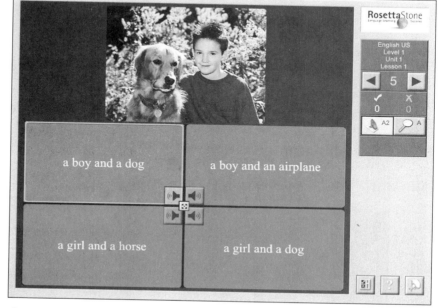

 Speaker buttons are located to the left of the prompt or in the center of the response options (pictured above).

- Click a speaker button to repeat a prompt or a response.

 - To hear all four response options, click the square in the middle of the four boxes.

You have as many chances as you need to answer correctly, except in the Test (2.10). Score is noted in all Exercises except Exercise 1 of Language Skill D: Speaking and Exercises 1 and 3 of Language Skill E: Writing. In a Test, the score is also saved. For more information, see Control Panel (2.12) and Test Scores (3.1.6).

2.9.2 Picture Exercises for Language Skill D: Speaking

The Exercise for Language Skill D follows a slightly different pattern than Language Skills A, B, and C. Instead of choosing between four answers, you repeat the spoken phrase.

To do an Exercise:

- Listen to the spoken phrase.
- After the phrase is spoken, the program automatically begins to record.

  To hear the spoken phrase again, click the top speaker button:
- Repeat the phrase exactly as you heard it. See page 16 for tips on how to improve your rating.

  Recording automatically stops when you are finished speaking. If it does not, click on the screen.
- Click the lower speaker button to hear your speech:
- Compare your Voiceprint with that of the native speaker. For more information on the Voiceprint, see the next page.
- Look at the Meter to see how closely you have imitated the native speaker. Red (on the left) is least accurate; green (on the right) is most accurate.

  To record the phrase again, click the record button:

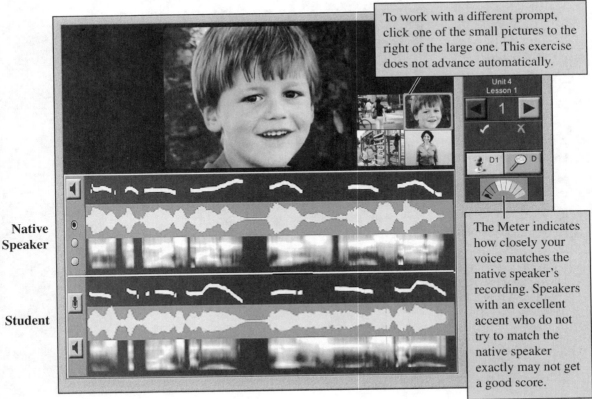

To work with a different prompt, click one of the small pictures to the right of the large one. This exercise does not advance automatically.

Native Speaker

Student

The Meter indicates how closely your voice matches the native speaker's recording. Speakers with an excellent accent who do not try to match the native speaker exactly may not get a good score.

Understanding the Voiceprint:

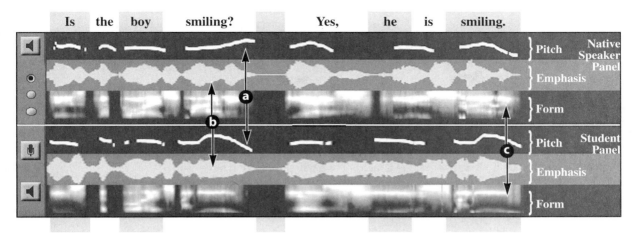

The Voiceprint allows you to compare your pronunciation with that of the native speaker. It displays:

- pitch (the rise and fall of the voice)
- emphasis (the stress on syllables and sounds)
- form (high and low sounds, where the tone resonates in your mouth and nose)

At **a,** the native speaker's voice rose in pitch, marking the end of a question, but the student's voice dropped.

At **b,** the native speaker stressed the first syllable in "smiling," but the student stressed the second syllable.

At **c,** the native speaker used the correct English vowel sound in the second syllable of "smiling," but the student used "ee."

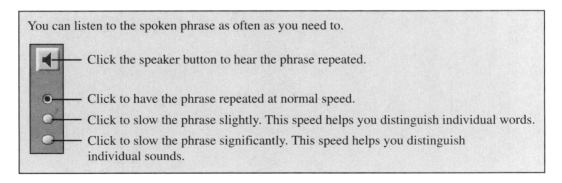

Note: If you are running Windows and your sound card is equipped with Microphone Gain Control, make sure the gain control is turned on inside the record controls panel.

continued on next page

To improve your rating:

- You may find speaking Exercises most helpful in the Lessons you have already worked with using the other Language Skills. Because the vocabulary and sentence structure are already familiar, you can focus on pronunciation and emphasis.

- The best way to perfect pronunciation is to focus on a relatively short phrase, repeating it many times.

- Keep background noise to a minimum.

- Pronounce beginning and ending sounds clearly. The program may ignore sounds if you let your voice drop at the end of a phrase.

- Adjust the distance between your mouth and the microphone to achieve the best recording volume. A headset with earphones and a microphone will produce the best results.

2.9.3 Picture Exercises for Language Skill E: Writing

The Exercises for Language Skill E follow a different pattern than the Exercises for Language Skills A, B, and C. Supply the response by arranging the tiles or by typing what you hear.

Exercises 1 and 2: Typing

To do an Exercise:

- Listen to the prompt and look at the picture it represents.
- Type the phrase using your computer's keyboard or the on-screen keyboard.

  The most common accents and characters are represented on the keyboard.

  If a character is not on the keyboard, click the pink key to reveal a special keyboard with other accents and characters.

- To check your answer, click the check answer icon:

  If your answer is correct, a new prompt will appear (Exercise 2) or you can click one of the four small pictures to the right of the large one (Exercise 1).

  If your answer is incorrect, the first incorrect character will be highlighted, and you can try again.

- To move to a new prompt without answering correctly, click the give up button [X▸] (Exercise 2), or click one of the four small pictures to the right of the large one (Exercise 1).

> Exercises 1 and 3 do not advance automatically. To work with a different prompt, click one of the small pictures to the right of the large one. To move to the next screen, click the right arrow.

Exercise 1

Prompt

Text Box

On-Screen Keyboard

> There are two difficulty settings for exercises 1 and 2:
>
> **Easy** (the default setting) does not require correct capitalization or punctuation.
>
> **Strict** requires correct capitalization and punctuation.
>
> Both settings require correctly accented characters. Select a setting difficulty by clicking the button of your choice.

continued on next page

Exercises 3 and 4: Tiles

To do an Exercise:

- Listen to the prompt and look at the picture it represents.

- Construct the phrase by clicking on the correct tiles.

  Click the beginning tile and it will appear in the text box below.

  Click the next tile and continue until the phrase or sentence is complete.

  To move a tile in the text box, click it or drag to the correct place.

  To delete a tile from the text box, click it. It will reappear with the other tiles above the text box.

- To check your answer, click the check answer icon: ✓?

  If your answer is correct, a new prompt will appear (Exercise 4) or you can click another picture (Exercise 3).

  If your answer is incorrect, the first incorrect tile will be highlighted, and you can try again.

- To move to a new prompt without answering correctly, click the give up button ☒▶ (Exercise 4) or click one of the four small pictures to the right of the large one (Exercise 3).

> For all Exercises, you have as many chances as you need to answer correctly, except in the Test (2.10). Exercises 1 and 3 are for practice and do not keep track of your score. Exercises 2 and 4 keep track of your score and are available as Tests. For more information about scoring, see Control Panel (2.12).
>
> **Note:** Some languages do not have all Writing Exercises.

Exercise 3

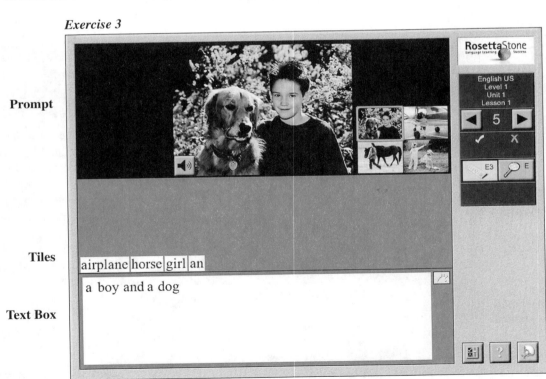

Prompt

Tiles

| airplane | horse | girl | an |

Text Box

a boy and a dog

2.9.4 End Screen

When you are finished with a Guided Exercise or Test, the End screen will appear:

This is the amount of time you took to do the Exercise.

0:04:53

Click on the left arrow to repeat the Lesson.

Repeat Lesson 01–01

Proceed to Lesson 01–02

Click on the right arrow to do the next Lesson in the same Exercise and Language Skill.

To do the next Lesson in a different Exercise or Language Skill, click on the right arrow while holding the command key (Macintosh) or the control key (Windows). This will take you to the Activities screen (2.5) of the next Lesson.

To do the same Lesson in a different Exercise or Language Skill, click on the bail out button to return to the Activities screen of the Lesson you have just done.

To return to the Menu screen (2.1), click on the bail-out button while holding both the shift key and the command key (Macintosh) or the shift key and control key (Windows).

2.10 Tests

The Test lets you to assess mastery of a Lesson by:

- allowing only one chance to click on the correct response.

- saving all Test Scores so you can chart your progress.

Your Test scores can be viewed from the Settings Panel (3.1.6).

Note: Test Scores will be kept only if you log in (3.1.1). If you are logged in as Guest, your Test Scores will not be recorded.

If the Test feature is on, the Test icon will appear to the right of each Exercise button.

To take a Test:

- Click the Test button:
- Then click the Exercise you wish to do.

2.11 Modes

Modes provide different ways to study the Lesson (2.4) material within a specific Language Skill (2.6) and Exercise (2.9).

All Modes can be turned on or off in the Activities screen (2.6).

The Modes are:
- Delay (2.11.1)
- Timer (2.11.2)

2.11.1 Delay Mode

In Delay Mode, you see, hear, or read the prompt, before the response options appear. After the prompt is given, it is hidden and the response options are given.

Use the Delay Mode to improve memory and comprehension.

To turn on Delay Mode:

- Click on the Delay button in the Control Panel of the Activities screen:
- Click the Exercise you wish to do.

To do an Exercise in Delay Mode:

- Hear, see, or read the prompt.
- Hear, see, or read the response options and select the correct one.

2.11.2 Timer

The Timer limits the amount of time in which you have to click on a response option. If you do not answer within the allotted time, the program automatically advances to the next question.

> **Note:** The Timer and Delay Mode can be used together to approximate the pace of real-life communication. Both can be used with Exercises or Tests.

To activate the Timer:

- Click the the Timer button:

- Set the time limit (1-60 seconds) by clicking on the arrows above and below the time, located beside the Timer button. Default time limit is 5 seconds.
- Click on the Exercise you wish to do.
- The countdown of the time limit begins when the prompt is complete.

Use the Timer to quicken comprehension and response time.

2.12 Control Panel

The Control Panel is always on the right side of the screen.

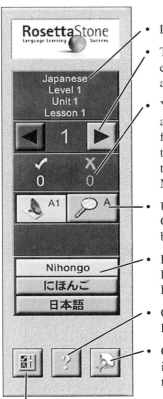

- Language, Product, Unit, and Lesson are always listed here.

- These arrows allow you to move between the quads or questions of a Lesson, except in a Test. Click the right arrow to move to the next screen and the left arrow to move to the previous screen.

- Your score is based on a 100 point scale. Both correct and incorrect answers are tallied. In the Picture Lessons, one quad is worth a total of 10 points. The first correct response is worth four points, second response is worth three points, the third response is worth two points, and one point for the last response. In the Video Lessons, each comprehension question is worth five points. In the Narrative Lessons, each comprehension question is worth ten points.

- Use the Preview/Exercise toggle to switch between the Preview and an Exercise. Click the Preview button (right) to enter Preview (2.7). Click the Exercise button (left) again to resume the Exercise.

- Four languages (Arabic, Chinese, Hebrew, and Japanese) have multiple Language Scripts. To use an alternate Language Script, click on the Language Script button of your choice.

- Click on the Help button to access the On-Screen Help Text at any time. For more information, see Getting Started (1.0).

- Click on the Bail Out button to return to the previous screen. For example, if you are in the middle of a Lesson, clicking on the Bail Out button will take you back to the Activities screen.

- Click on the Settings Panel button to change the program settings. For more information, see Program Settings (3.0).

In the Preview, you can also use the Control Panel to:

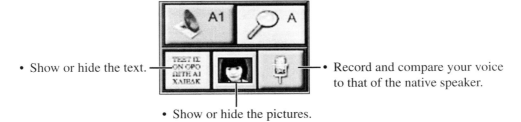

- Show or hide the text.
- Record and compare your voice to that of the native speaker.
- Show or hide the pictures.

See Preview (2.7) for more informtion.

3.0 Program Settings

In this section, you can learn how to adjust the program settings, which is done with the Settings Panel.

- Open the Settings Panel by clicking the settings button, located in the bottom right corner of the Control Panel (2.12).

If you are logged in (3.1.1), any changes to the program settings will be saved, but will take effect only when *you* are logged in. If you are logged in as Guest, any changes you make will become the default program settings.

3.1 User Options Tab

The User Options tab is the top tab in the Settings Panel.

- Open the Settings Panel by clicking the Settings button, located in the bottom right corner of the screen.
- The Settings Panel opens directly to the User Options tab.

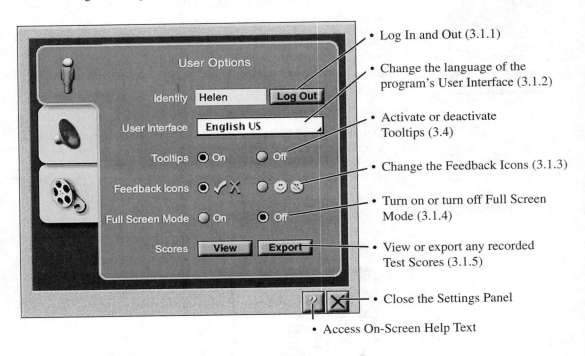

- Log In and Out (3.1.1)
- Change the language of the program's User Interface (3.1.2)
- Activate or deactivate Tooltips (3.4)
- Change the Feedback Icons (3.1.3)
- Turn on or turn off Full Screen Mode (3.1.4)
- View or export any recorded Test Scores (3.1.5)
- Close the Settings Panel
- Access On-Screen Help Text

3.1.1 Logging In and Out

The Login screen appears when you first open the program. You may also log in or out at any time by opening the Settings Panel (3.0) to the User Options tab (3.1).

- Open the Settings Panel by clicking the Settings button, located in the bottom right corner of the screen.

- The Settings Panel opens directly to the User Options tab.

In User Options:

- Click the Log In button, located beside the Identity field.

- This will bring up the Login screen.

To log in under a Username:

- Type your name in the Username field and click OK.

- If you have logged in before, you can find your Username listed by clicking on Guest (below the Username box). A pull-down menu will appear.

- Drag the mouse cursor over your Username and click on it.

  There is a limit of 15 stored Usernames per computer.

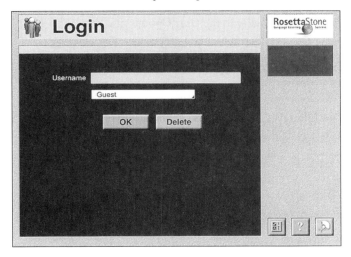

When you log in, you create a user profile. This means:

- Your Test Scores (2.10, 3.1.6) will be saved.

- Changes to program settings (3.0) will be saved (for example, Volume level or choice of Feedback Icons).

To delete a user profile, select the Username and click on the Delete button.

continued on next page

To log in as a Guest:

- Leave the Username field blank and click OK.

If you log in as Guest:

- You can change default program settings.
- Your Test Scores (2.10) will not be saved.
- Your place in the program will not be saved.

To log out:

- Open the Settings Panel to the User Options tab.
- Click the Log Out button, located beside the Identity field.
- The Identity field should now read "Not logged in."

3.1.2 User Interface Language

The User Interface Language is the language in which components of the program, screen titles, and Tooltips appear. For example, the words "Unit," "Activities," and "Guided Exercise" are all part of the User Interface.

To access the User Interface Language settings:

- Open the Settings Panel by clicking the Settings button, located in the bottom right corner of the screen.
- The Settings Panel opens directly to the User Options tab.
- The User Interface setting is the second item on the User Options tab.

To change the User Interface Language:

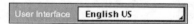

- Click on the User Interface Language box. All the available languages will appear.
- Click on the language you wish to use.

The default User Interface Language is English.

3.1.3 Tooltips

Tooltips are small labels that appear when you let the mouse rest on certain buttons in the program.

To access the Tooltips setting:

- Open the Settings Panel by clicking the Settings button, located in the bottom right corner of the screen.
- The Settings Panel opens directly to the User Options tab.
- The Tooltips setting is the third item on the User Options tab.

To turn the Tooltips on or off:

- Click the button of your choice.

3.1.4 Feedback Icons

The Feedback Icons indicate whether the answers you select in an Exercise are correct or incorrect.

To access the Feedback Icons setting:

- Open the Settings Panel by clicking the Settings button, located in the bottom right corner of the screen.

- The Settings Panel opens directly to the User Options tab.

- The Feedback Icons setting is the fourth item on the User Options tab.

To choose a set of Feedback Icons:

- Click on the button beside the pair of your choice.

3.1.5 Full Screen Mode

You can choose whether you want the Rosetta Stone to:

- cover the entire screen (Full Screen Mode).

- run in a window allowing you to see your desktop or other programs.

> **Note:** To run the program in a window, your screen resolution must be higher than 800 x 600.

To access the Full Screen Mode setting:

- Open the Settings Panel by clicking the Settings button, located in the bottom right corner of the screen.

- The Settings Panel opens directly to the User Options tab.

- The Full Screen Mode setting is the fifth item on the User Options tab.

To turn Full Screen Mode on or off:

- Click the button of your choice.

3.1.6 Test Scores

To access Test Scores:

- Open the Settings Panel by clicking the Settings button, located in the bottom right corner of the screen.

- The Settings Panel opens directly to the User Options tab.

- The options for accessing Test Scores are the sixth item on the User Options tab. If you do not see the Score line, you need to log in and take the Test again. For more information, see Test (2.10) and Logging In and Out (3.1.1).

> You can save and access Test Scores only if:
>
> - you are logged in (3.1.1).
>
> - you have taken at least one Test (2.10) while logged in.

To view Test Scores:

View allows you to look at your Test Scores with a web browser.

- Simply click View. You will be taken directly to your Test Scores.

To export Test Scores:

Export allows you to save your Test Scores as a text or HTML file.

- Text file: standard ASCII file, which can be viewed or printed from any text editor or word processor.
- HTML file: can be viewed in a web browser.
- Click Export.
- Choose a place to save the file (the hard drive or a removable disk).
- Click save for both the HTML and text files.
- The Test Score files will appear where you saved them and may be opened, e-mailed, or printed.

3.2 Sound Options Tab

The Sound Options tab is the middle tab in the Settings Panel.

- Open the Settings Panel by clicking the Settings button, located in the bottom right corner of the screen.

- Click the second tab.

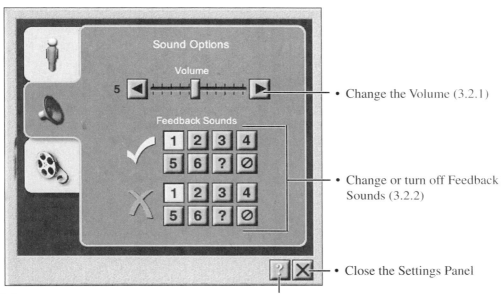

- Change the Volume (3.2.1)

- Change or turn off Feedback Sounds (3.2.2)

- Close the Settings Panel

- Access On-Screen Help Text

3.2.1 Volume

To access the Volume setting:

- Open the Settings Panel by clicking the Settings button, located in the bottom right corner of the screen.

- Click the Sound Options tab.

- The Volume setting is the first item on the Sound Options tab.

To raise the Volume:

- Click the slider, located on the volume bar, and drag it to the right.
  or
- Click the right arrow (beside the volume bar).

To lower the Volume:

- Click the slider and drag it to the left.
  or
- Click the left arrow (beside the volume bar).

3.2.2 Feedback Sounds

Feedback Sounds indicate whether the response options you click on are correct or incorrect. Choose between six "correct" sounds and six "incorrect" sounds, or turn them off completely.

To access the Feedback Sounds setting:

- Open the Settings Panel by clicking the Settings button, located in the bottom right corner of the screen.

- Click the Sound Options tab.

- The Feedback Sounds setting is the second item on the Sound Options tab.

To change the Feedback Sounds:

- Click on a numbered button to select the Feedback Sound.
- Click ? to hear Feedback Sounds at random as you answer questions.
- Click ⊘ to turn the Feedback Sounds off.

3.3 Level 3 Options Tab

The Level 3 Options tab is the bottom tab in the Settings Panel. It contains options unique to Level 3 that do not apply to any other product.

4.0 Reference

The reference section contains the following sections:
- System Requirements (4.1)
- Troubleshooting (4.2)
- Technical Support Contact Information (4.3)
- Glossary of Commonly Used Terms (4.4)
- Glossary of Icons and Graphics (4.3)
  - Index (4.5)

4.1 System Requirements Levels 1 and 2: CD-ROM

Windows
Minimum
- Windows 95/98/Me or NT 4.0/2000 or XP
- Pentium 233 MHz processor
- 64 MB RAM (96 MB for 2000 or XP)
- 35 MB free hard drive space
- 4X CD-ROM drive
- 16-bit Windows compatible sound card
- Microphone (for voice recognition exercises)

Recommended
- Windows 98/Me/XP
- Pentium 350 MHz processor
- 128 MB RAM
- 35 MB free hard drive space
- 16X CD-ROM drive
- 32-bit color display or better
- SoundBlaster 16 card or better
- Headset microphone

Mac OS
Minimum
- Mac OS 8.6 or later (requires Classic Mode for OS X)
- PowerPC G3 233 MHz processor
- 64 MB free RAM (96 MB for OS X)
- 35 MB free hard drive space
- 4X CD-ROM drive
- PlainTalk compatible microphone (for voice recognition exercises)

Recommended
- Mac OS 9.0.4 or later (including OS X)
- PowerPC G3 400 MHz processor
- 128 MB RAM
- 35 MB free hard drive space
- 16X CD-ROM drive
- 32-bit color display or better
- PlainTalk compatible microphone or headset microphone

4.2 Troubleshooting

4.2.1 Sound

If there is no sound when you run the Rosetta Stone program:

- Make sure Volume (3.9) for the program is set above zero.
- Make sure the volume for the computer operating system is set above zero, and that mute is turned off.
- If there is still no sound:

Windows 98:

1. Open the Multimedia Control Panel, Audio tab.
2. Select "Use only preferred devices."
3. Click OK.

> This section addresses the most common problems in running the Rosetta Stone, but is not comprehensive. For answers to more issues, see section 4.2 of the On-Screen Help Text.

Windows 2000:

Note: The following will disable your modem as a sound device, but will not affect your modem as a communication device.

1. Open the Sounds and Multimedia Control Panel.
2. Click on the Hardware tab.
3. Highlight the modem device.
3. Click Properties. The Unimodem Half-Duplex Audio Device Properties window will appear.
4. Reopen the Unimodem Half-Duplex Audio Device Properties window and click on the Properties tab.
5. Open Audio Devices.
6. Highligh "Modem Wave Driver."
7. Click the Properties button.
8. Select "Do Not Map Through This Divice."
9. Click OK.

Mac OS

Open the Sound Control Panel and make sure the appropriate output device is selected.

If the sound is bad:

- you may need to update your sound card drivers. Check the Web site of the manufacturer of your comuputer or the manufacturer of your sound card for updated audio drivers.
- your sound card may be incompatible with the Rosetta Stone. Please contact Technical Support (4.3).

4.2.2 Recording

If the voice recording does not work in the Rosetta Stone program:

- If you are using an external microphone, make sure it is plugged into the correct port or jack.

Windows

- Click on Start: Programs: Accessories: Entertainment: Volume Control.
- Click on Options: Properties.
- Select Recording.
- Check all the boxes in the lower part of the window.
- Click OK.
- Make sure the microphone is turned up and the Select box is checked.

Mac OS

- Open the Sound Control Panel.
- Make sure the appropriate input device is selected.

If the recording does not stop after you have stopped speaking:

- Make sure there is no background noise.
- Isolate the microphone from computer noise or vibration.
- You may have to stop the recording manually by clicking once anywhere on the screen.

If the recording playback has a lot of static:

- Try another microphone.
- You may need to update your sound card drivers. Check the website of the manufacturer of your computer or the manufacturer of your sound card for updated audio drivers.
- Your sound card may not be compatible with the Rosetta Stone. Please contact Technical Support (4.3).

4.3 Technical Support Information

 The On-line Help Text contains the information included in this book. You can access it at http://www.RosettaStone.com/home/support or by clicking on the help button, located in the bottom right corner of the screen, at any time.

If you need further assistance, please contact the tech support team at Fairfield Language Technologies.

Call   1-800-788-0822 (toll-free) or 1-540-432-6166
           Live technical support hours: M-F 9am-6pm EST

Fax   1-540-432-0953

Write 135 W. Market St.
           Harrisonburg, VA 22801 USA

Email support@RosettaStone.com

For further information,
- email: info@RosettaStone.com
- or visit our website: http://www.RosettaStone.com

4.4 Glossary of Terms and Icons

Activities Screen: The screen that appears after you select a Lesson. It allows you to select the Language Skill, Exercise, and Mode.

application: The program that actually runs the Rosetta Stone. The application needs to be installed before the language data disc can be used.

application disc: The disc which contains the application program. Often this is separate from the language data disc, but in some cases the application and language data are on the same disc.

Bail Out button: A button in lower right corner of every screen. Click on this to go back to the previous screen. If you are in an Exercise or Test, the Bail Out button will take you back to the Activities screen. If you are at the menu screen, the Bail Out button allows you to exit the Rosetta Stone program.

Control Panel: The block of information and buttons in the upper right corner of every screen.

difficulty levels: Settings for Exercises 1 and 2 of Language Skill E: Writing, located to the right of the text box. Easy (the default) does not require correct capitalization or punctuation. Strict requires correct capitalization and punctuation.

Delay Mode: A way to modify any Exercise for Language Skills A, B, and C. In Delay Mode, the response options are hidden while the prompt is given. After the prompt is given, it disappears and the response options appear.

Delay button: Located in the Control Panel of the Activities screen. Click on it to activate or deactivate Delay Mode.

End screen: The screen that appears when you have completed a Guided Exercise, Exercise, or Test. It allows you to repeat the exercise or Test you have just completed, or to move to other Lessons, Language Skills, or Exercises.

Exercise: Ways of working with the Lesson material within different Language Skills. The core Activities of the Rosetta Stone program, Exercises teach through combinations of visual, spoken, and written prompts and response options. Level 3 offers Picture, Video, and Narrative exercises; all other products use Picture Exercises only.

Exercise button: Click on this button, located in the Activities screen, to select the Exercise it represents. Each Exercise button indicates what combinations of picture, written text, and speech will be used in the prompts and response options for that particular Exercise.

Exercise/Preview toggle: A set of two side-by-side buttons in the Control Panel of the Preview and Exercises that allows you to move between the Preview (represented by a magnifying glass) and the Exercise (represented by the symbol for Language Skill A).

Export Test Scores: This button allows you to save and view your Test Scores outside the program, as either a text file or an HTML file.

Feedback Icons: Pictures that indicate whether your response is correct or incorrect. You can change the Feedback Icons in the Settings Panel.

Feedback Sounds: Sounds that indicate whether your response is correct or incorrect. You can change or turn off the Feedback Sounds in the Settings Panel.

Full Screen Mode: An option that allows you to run the Rosetta Stone over the entire screen or as a window. Located in the User Options tab of the Settings Panel.

give up button: The red X beside the text box in Picture Exercises 3 and 4 for Language Skill E: Writing. Click on this to advance to the next prompt without answering the question.

Guided Exercise: A way of working with the Lesson material within different Language Skills. The Guided Exercise allows you to work through the lesson material with a combination of all Exercises and Modes available in that Language Skill.

Guest: The default Username of the Rosetta Stone program. You can either log in as Guest or choose a different Username and create a user profile. The Guest log in allows you to change program settings, but Test results will not be saved.

Help button: The middle of three buttons in the lower right corner of every screen. Click on this to open a Web browser window with the On-Screen Help Text; you will be taken to the help section(s) concerning the screen with which you are working.

Identity field: The space in the User Options tab that indicates if anyone is logged in and, if so, which user.

Language: The language being taught with the Rosetta Stone program. Indicated in the top line of the Control Panel.

language data disc: The language information component of the Rosetta Stone program. Sometimes it is a disc separate from the application, while in other cases the application and language data are on the same CD-ROM. After you have installed the application, insert this disc to use the program.

Language Skill: Five approaches to the Lesson material. Each emphasizes different elements of communication. They are A: Listening and Reading, B: Listening, C: Reading, D: Speaking, E: Writing.

Language Skill tab: The tabs on the left of the Activities screen. Click on one to look at the Exercises taught in that Language Skill.

Lesson: A manageable, structured sequence of language material that acts as a building block within the Rosetta Stone. Lesson material is studied through the Language Skills, Preview, Guided Exercise, Exercises, Tests, and Modes.

Level 3 Options tab: The third tab on the left of the Settings Panel. Click on its icon to change program settings unique to Level 3: the Video's Background Music Volume, the Text Size, activate or deactivate the glossary, and activate or deactivate AutoScrolling.

Login screen: The screen, accessed through the User Options tab of the Settings Panel, which allows you to log in under a user profile or as a Guest, change to a different user profile, and create or delete a user profile.

Menu screen: The screen where you can choose the Language (in some cases), Product, Unit, and Lesson with which you would like to work. It appears after you log in.

Meter: The color-coded fan located directly below the exercise/preview toggle switch in Picture Exercises for Language Skill D: Speaking. The Meter indicates how closely your voice matches that of the native speaker.

microphone icon: Click this button to record your own voice. This feature is available in the Preview and in Language Skill D: Speaking.

Mode: Two ways—Delay and/or Timer—to modify the way you work with the Lesson material in an Exercise or Test.

On-Screen Help Text: A virtual version of the User's Guide that is linked to the program. Access the On-Screen Help Text at any time by clicking on the help button, located in the bottom right corner of any screen. You will be taken directly to a relevant section in the On-Screen Help Text. You can also click on words within the On-Screen Help Text to move to a different topic in the document.

on-screen keyboard: The keyboard layout appears in Exercises 1 and 2 of Language Skill E: Writing. The on-screen keyboard shows which keyboard buttons correspond with which characters in the target language.

picture button: One of three buttons available in the Preview, located directly below the preview/exercise toggle switch. Click on the picture button to hide or reveal the pictures.

Preview: A way of working with the Lesson material. The Preview allows you to study the answers: to see and hear the text matched with the correct picture. You can also practice reading and listening comprehension and pronunciation. Score is not kept in the Preview.

Preview button: Click on this button, located in the Activities screen, to select the Preview.

Product: A collection of units which make up a version of the Rosetta Stone program. Current products are Level 1, Level 2, and Level 3. Not all Products are available in each Language. Level 3 offers Picture, Video, and Narrative Units; all other Products use Picture Units only.

Program Settings: Changes you can make to the environment of the Rosetta Stone. The program settings include Volume, Feedback Sounds and Icons, and the User Interface Language. All program settings can be changed in the Settings Panel.

prompt: A picture, speech, written text, or any combination of the three. When a prompt appears in an exercise, select the appropriate response.

record button: One of three buttons available in the Preview, located directly under the exercise/preview toggle. Click on this to open the microphone so that you can record your own pronunciation and compare it to that of the native speaker.

response option: Four pictures, text, speech, or combinations of the three that appear below the prompt (in Picture Lessons) or the question (in Video and Narrative Lessons). One of these response options matches the prompt. Click on it to get the answer correct and move to the next prompt.

scene: A small section of the video that is studied as a single lesson.

scene selection bar: A row of numbered buttons directly below the video screen in a Video Lesson. Each button corresponds to a scene in the video. Click on a number to move to the corresponding scene.

Score: The correct and incorrect answers you have given in an Exercise. A perfect score is 100. In a quad, the first correct answer is worth four points, the second worth three, the third worth two, and the fourth worth one. However, the first incorrect answer costs four points, and so on.

settings button: The leftmost of three buttons at the lower right corner of every screen, showing a check mark, an "X" and a slide bar, that takes you to the Settings Panel.

Settings Panel: A window that presents options for program settings. It is has three tabs: the User Options tab, the Sound Options tab, and the Level 3 Options tab. It is accessed by clicking on the settings button, located in the lower right corner of every screen.

speaker button: Click on this to hear a speech again.

Test: A way of working with the Lesson material within different Language Skills. The Test function allows you to gauge your progress and check your knowledge of the Language within the various Exercises.

Test Scores: The correct answers you gave while taking a Test, the points, and the elapsed time of the test. These are saved only when you are logged in and have taken a Test. You can access Test Scores in the User Options tab of the Control Panel.

text button: One of three buttons available in the Preview, located directly below the preview/exercise toggle switch. Click on the text button to hide or reveal the text.

Text Size: The text of the scripts (in the Video Lessons) and the questions for both units may be viewed in three sizes. Adjust the Text Size in the Level 3 Options tab of the Settings Panel.

tiles: Used in Exercises 1 and 2 of Language Skill E: Writing. These are blocks, each with a word or punctuation mark written on it. After hearing the prompt, you must choose and arrange the tiles to write what you have just heard.

time limit: In Timer Mode, the amount of time you have to answer a question before it is counted incorrect. You can turn the Timer on by clicking on the timer button located in the Control Panel of the Activities screen. You can set the time limit by clicking on the up or down arrows beside the timer button. The default time limit is 5 seconds.

Timer: A Mode in which you can run the Exercises or Test. The Timer will count an answer incorrect and move to the next prompt if you do not answer within the allotted time limit.

Timer button: One of three buttons located on the Control Panel directly above the exercise/preview toggle. Click this button to activate the Timer.

Tooltips: Small labels that appear when you rest the mouse cursor on a button or feature. You can turn these off or on in the User Options tab of the Settings Panel.

Unit: Collections of Lessons. A Product is divided into Units, which are divided into Lessons. In Level 3, there are three kinds of Units: Picture, Video, and Narrative. In all other Products, there are Picture Units only.

User Interface: The words that label the different screens (Menu, Activities) and features (Exercise, Preview, Guided Exercise) in the program.

User Interface Language: The language in which the User Interface is written. You can change this in the User Options tab of the Settings Panel.

User Options tab: The first tab in the Settings Panel. Use the User Options tab to log in and out, change the User Interface Language, activate or deactivate Tooltips, change the Feedback Icons, turn on or turn off Full Screen Mode, and access Test Scores if available.

Username field: The space where you type your name when logging in.

user profile: An account in the program. You can create one by logging in. The user profile will store any changes you have made to settings, any Test Scores, and will remember where you left off.

View Test Scores: This option allows you to view your Test Scores in a web browser. You can find it in the User Options tab of the Settings Panel. To view Test Scores, you must have taken a test while logged in and you must currently be logged in.

Voiceprint: The chart in the Exercise for Language Skill D: Speaking that shows pitch, form, and tone of speech. The top section displays the pitch, form, and tone of the native speaker. The bottom section displays those of the student's recorded speech.

Volume: How loud or quiet the speech and Feedback sounds are. You can adjust the Volume in the Sound Options tab of the Settings Panel.

volume bar: The bar, numbered from one to ten, that shows the Volume setting in the Sound Options tab of the Settings Panel.

4.5 Index